# EXTRAORDINARY

# LOVE

## FAITH-BASED PARENTING
## FOR SPECIAL NEEDS KIDS

# BOBBY LANYON

*Extraordinary Love* by Bobby Lanyon
Copyright © 2016 by Bobby Lanyon
All Rights Reserved.
ISBN: 978-1-59755-409-1

Published by: ADVANTAGE BOOKS™
Longwood, Florida, USA
www.advbookstore.com

Library of Congress Catalog Number: 2016945682


Also available in all eBook formats:
eBook ISBN: 9781597554145



First Printing: August 2016
16 17 18 19 20 21 22     10 9 8 7 6 5 4 3 2 1
Printed in the United States of America

*To Michelle, BJ, Jack and Connor.*

*Thank you for inspiring me to pursue being the husband and dad whom God wants me to be for you.*

*Bobby Lanyon*

# Foreword

"God is too good to be unkind and too wise to make a mistake." This is a theological sentiment most believers in God would affirm. It is a challenge, nevertheless, when your family is hit with a seeming anomaly: a special needs child who appears to be facing life with unfair difficulties. The author of this helpful book and his wife have weathered such a theological and practical challenge. From their own experiences, further study, and application of biblical principles, they recommend that those who face similar issues consider the various aspects of human existence that will need attention with the addition of a special needs child to the family circle and the practical steps that can be taken to ensure the best possible experience for all involved. "Let the little children come unto Me, and forbid them not" was the command of Jesus of Nazareth as He ministered in this world. We are not misunderstanding His statement when we insist He certainly meant all of them!

-- Dr. Tom Davis, Academic Dean, Word of Life Bible Institute

*Bobby Lanyon*

# Table of Contents

# Introduction

People who play sports together often have camaraderie that extends beyond the field, a lifelong friendship from the common bond of being on the same team and sharing the same experiences. I've found a similar bond among parents of children with special needs. It really doesn't matter what the diagnosis is: autism, Asperger's, Down syndrome, spina bifida, cerebral palsy, or any other life-changing disorder. This brotherhood and sisterhood brings with it a mutual understanding of a new way of life that will forever include weekly therapy, seasons of constant visits to doctors and medical specialists, and sometimes heart-wrenching surgeries on helpless bodies.

Living in this world automatically gives a mom or dad the credibility to say "I understand" to another struggling parent — and the struggling parent can know they really do.

This special needs community has been used by God in my family's time of need to provide support, encouragement, advice, wisdom, and direction. Yet we found one critical aspect was missing: a faith-based approach to our life. As my family sought godly advice in raising our child with special needs, we felt lonely because much of the material written for godly parenting is intended for typically developing children. The question I kept asking myself was: "How does this apply to my son?" The answer often was: It doesn't. The traditional teaching doesn't fully address the unique needs of my son — and even of us, as parents — however well-meaning.

Finally, after much prayer and conversations with godly men, the Lord sent my wife and me on this amazing adventure of articulating how to have a biblical perspective and purpose while parenting a child with special needs.

The goal of this study is to help create a paradigm through which we can filter instruction, advice, comments, and research in a biblical fashion.

From the outset, I want to make clear that this is not intended to be a play-by-play book or a methodology of parenting. Focusing on parenting methodology is difficult simply because the challenges of each diagnosis vary greatly. But I pray that the content of the following pages will instead give us a purpose and end goal for how God wants us to parent our kids with disabilities. How you choose to implement these principles is entirely your privilege and wholly your responsibility as the parent of your child. I pray God will give us the wisdom to understand and act on the truth from the Bible that follows.

*Bobby Lanyon*

# Chapter One

## Congratulations or Sorry

*How other people respond to meeting your child may not be how God responds*

My wife, Michelle, and I have the pleasure of raising three boys and a dog. Only two years after our wedding day, I had the awesome privilege of witnessing my wife give birth. If you've been in the delivery room, you know it's something you can never forget. It truly is the most amazing miracle. No matter what's in the news that day, you're not going to remember it once your child is born. Birth is a life-changing event that fills you with pride, joy, and a mixture of anxiety and feeling immortal — at least until the doctor pulls you aside and tells you your child has a disability.

That's the conversation you vividly remember. Whether it was prenatal or after birth, it will never leave you. I hope you were blessed with a doctor with an understanding and compassionate bedside manner. We were not.

It was a cool early morning in late January 2009 when our second son, Jackson, was born with a 9.8 Apgar score. I remember the nurse handing Jackson to me, and my first words to him caused a response I'll never forget. After I welcomed him into this world, he reached out and touched my chin. I knew we had a bond. Although he had trouble feeding, he was full-term and ready for life.

The following day, however, my wife awoke to learn that during the night Jackson had been transferred to the Neonatal Intensive Care Unit. On that unforgettable day, we were callously informed that Jackson has Trisomy 21, otherwise known as Down syndrome, which was confirmed seven days later courtesy of a karyotype.

As we stood in the Neonatal Intensive Care Unit, the world seemed to stop. My wife fell into my arms in tears, concluding from what we knew so far that Jackson might not even live to make it home.

After the initial shock, two weeks in the hospital, much reading, asking questions, and encouragement from close family, it was time to return to everyday life.

At this point, the public reality of having a child with a disability became more evident. This was when the comments started to come. You've probably heard them yourself. When news travels that your fresh bundle of joy has an intellectual or cognitive delay, well-intentioned friends and family often say in a well-intentioned, loving way, "I'm sorry."

Why were they saying this to me? Were they sorry because they thought Jack would not amount to anything? Were they sorry because they knew he would have extra struggles in life? Did they say "sorry" because they saw his diagnosis as bad news? Or were they saying "I'm sorry" because they really didn't know what else to say? Whatever their intentions, those two words conveyed that my child did not carry the same value of life as other children. After a while, I didn't even want it to come up in conversation that Jackson had Down syndrome, because I didn't want him to be pitied or judged based on his diagnosis. Perhaps you have been there.

I started to seriously search for God's perspective toward my child during this time. I kept saying to God, "God, you made Jack. Why do people have this response when they learn he has a disability?" Was I one of only a few people who viewed my child as amazingly awesome? Really? I grew up being taught all life is valuable and created by God. Was this wrong? I mean, let's be honest: Even people in our churches and faith-based communities respond this way. It's painful for parents who long for their child to be loved and accepted to keep hearing these comments from the people they look to for support and encouragement.

## SUCCESS" IN OUR CULTURE

So, let's figure out why people would respond this way. What logic could possibly cause people to be remorseful that we have children with disabilities rather than loving, supporting, and seeing our children as valuable and worthy of life?

I would like to suggest that people do not know how to approach someone with special needs because of a subconscious, unbiblical worldview that presupposes that individuals with special needs do not have a high quality of life.

This worldview comes from our culture. In western society, quality of life is equated with success — or, more specifically, what our culture considers success. For example, our culture has measures of success for business (earnings and profit), families (parents and kids who never disagree or struggle), or fashion (the latest clothes, and different ones every day). These measures of success are external and determined by people. Furthermore, success is presented in a way that says the people who meet these standards have a higher quality of life. Simply put, this worldview tells people: The more you succeed, the better your life is, and the better you are.

This way of thinking manifests itself in many ways in our culture. While some people buy into it more obviously, we all experience it to some degree. Even Christians are not immune to judging success and quality of life by these relative cultural standards. Many of us long for the bigger home, the fancier vacation, the newer car, or the elite school for our kids. Each of us personally has an idea of that external "something" that will make life better, whether it's a new job or hobby, an upgrade in our surroundings, or a situation working out the way we want.

While God certainly puts desires in our hearts and loves to bless us, there's something to be said for how this worldview can seep in and change the foundation of how we see and judge success, life, God, and ourselves. It's not just about wanting the new car; it's about how this way of thinking and what it considers important can redefine how we view people.

This worldview places the value of life and worth of people on what they can do, achieve, or attain — which is simply not biblical.

The Bible tells us all people have great value because they have been created in the image of God. Life itself is of great worth, and Scripture is full of examples of God recognizing the value of human life — no matter how "small" — and preserving it. Life consists of so much more than we can see, and a "better life" is found in a relationship with God and all He gives us.

In our culture's worldview, though, the better life belongs to those who "succeed" externally, meaning those who don't succeed in those terms have inferior lives and therefore are inferior people. The waitress is not worth as much as the CEO, and the teenager who doesn't get good grades isn't as valuable as the honor student. On and on it goes according to the various measures of success — and you can see where children with special needs end up in this way of thinking. Because this view of success is built on very measurable, external standards, people are very quickly classified, and limitations and differences are seen as drawbacks to their potential.

This is important for us to verbalize as Christians, and especially as Christian parents of children with special needs. If we place our faith in Christ for salvation and believe His truth in Scripture, we must also recognize that this man-made criteria of success is not biblical. We often don't realize we've taken on the world's idea of success, and we may forget how different God's perspective is. When we see clearly how our culture thinks compared to how God sees us and our children, it is easier for us to hope, to acknowledge and pursue biblical truth, and to find our way.

## THE BIBLE'S VIEW

Now that we've talked a little about our culture and its idea of success, let's look deeper at what the Bible has to say.

1 Samuel 16:7 tells us people look at outward appearances, but God looks at hearts. John 10:10 says abundant life comes through Jesus. Matthew 6:19-20 calls us to pursue heavenly treasures, which can't be destroyed, rather than earthly ones.

The Bible repeatedly teaches about the transience of this world and cautions people not to put their hope in what will pass away. James 4:14 tells us that even long, rich lives are like a disappearing vapor from eternity's perspective. 1 Corinthians 3:19 says the wisdom of this world is foolishness to God, and Romans 12:2 encourages us not to follow the world's way of thinking but instead to watch our lives change as our minds increasingly see life God's way.

Jesus was constantly comparing what people thought was important with what God says matters. He told the rich young ruler to forget his possessions and follow Him (Mark 10:17-27). When the young man found this too difficult, Jesus said it's easier for a camel to go through the eye of a needle than for the wealthy to enter the kingdom of God — a pretty big indictment of this world's view of success. Jesus' disciples were "amazed" when He said this. They, like many of us, judged people by what they could do, achieve, or attain in life. If the most "successful" people couldn't gain

Heaven, who could? A similar disconnect unfolds in Mark 10:37 when the disciples fight over a prominent position in the coming kingdom. Money, status, appearances — Jesus was dealing with a cultural worldview that was just as misguided as ours.

What we're seeing here is that the Bible doesn't just talk about success — the Bible actually redefines the *idea* of success. People think success has everything to do with what they do or accomplish (their physical, external, or earthly condition), but the Bible — and especially the message of Jesus Christ — says success is actually about the heart (inside, spiritual condition). The entire Bible seeks to draw attention to the spiritual and how God wants to have a relationship with each of us. When Jesus came, He gave even more specifics about what "succeeding" spiritually looks like — and even how His salvation in the spiritual realm has led and is leading to physical change and restoration.

This may sound like the Sunday School answer you've heard so many times, but it's very important to really grasp and internalize it. Understanding this is the crux of all Christian living, meaning it's essential not only to you as a parent of a child with special needs but also to you personally. The Bible doesn't teach a *different* way of success. That is, the world says to do a certain amount or achieve a certain thing to be successful, but the Bible doesn't offer an alternative "do" or "achieve." Instead, God's Word redefines the very *idea* of success. The Bible says success is found in a right relationship with God, which is a state of being. Even more, it's a state of being that is dependent on God and what He does in us, not anything we can do or achieve. That's why following God and His idea of success is so radical. There is no reaching or attaining. The people who know how to succeed by the world's standards have no advantage. The only thing you have to do to have a relationship with God is to be alive and to place your trust in Christ's work on the cross. The Gospel and God's idea of success go hand in hand because God has been trying to redefine our idea of success since the Fall — and all it takes to "succeed" is a relationship with Him.

Understanding this is especially comforting for parents of children with special needs because, unlike in our culture's worldview, we can know the God Who made our children has already equipped them for full success. Our children are in no way disadvantaged when it comes to what really matters in life.

Jesus taught on this a lot. In fact, many times He used children as an example of what was needed to enter the kingdom of Heaven. The faith of a child — untainted by the concerns of worldly success — was His model of how we should approach God. Jesus loved children and never treated them as if their youth or lack of achievement disqualified them from knowing Him. He even told adults to be more like them. The Jesus we see in the New Testament clearly would have loved the company of children with special needs.

Jesus also cautioned that too much attention on earthly advancements can keep people from seeing what's really important. Matthew 16:24-26 asks what good it is if a person gains the whole world but loses his or her soul. In Luke 12:16-21, a man wants to tear down his barns and build new, bigger ones to accommodate all his stuff — without giving any thought to his soul's destination if he dies that night. The other side is Matthew 13:44, where a man gives up everything he owns for a treasure he finds in a field (salvation through Christ), and that treasure is worth it. While many people see success — even in small measures — as their ticket to a better life, the Bible teaches that success can often inhibit us from finding what we really need. That's what Jesus was getting at with the Sermon on the Mount, where He contrasted many ideas of religious success with God's truth.

Religious "success," which also is very external, can be just as dangerous and demanding as worldly "success." Jesus turned the attention away from what people typically consider proper living and instead encouraged a lifestyle that requires dependence on God. The poor in spirit, the humble, those who weep — these people have little obstructing them from coming to God and resting in His strength. In the same way, the challenges we face as parents of children with special needs are often the gateway to knowing God better, even if we may seem to fall short of our culture's success standards.

## QUALITY OF LIFE

If we are not bound by our culture's definitions of success, we are free to follow God and what He says is important. This brings us back to quality of life. The world tells us quality of life comes from what people are able to do or how they can better themselves. The religious view, like our culture, also says quality of life depends on what we do, although it focuses on "spiritual" endeavors.

Those are typical ways of looking at success and quality of life that make sense in our achievement-oriented brains. But the Bible teaches something different. Scripture shows us God loves life — just life itself.

This is a different way of considering quality of life. It recognizes that God, when He created the world, took great joy just in creating life and people — with no to-do lists in their hands. God is glorified simply by life itself, and the life all around us reflects its Creator and gives Him glory just by being. God is glorified by people even if they can't "do something" for Him. This is real quality of life. This is what gives people so much worth. They have been created by a relational God Who knows each of them, and their simply being alive is valuable to Him and glorifies Him.

Everyone has a high quality of life, regardless of aptitude or abilities.

The Bible assures us that God not only was actively involved in the creation of the world but also is there in the formation of every life. In Psalm 119:73, the writer says, *"Your hands made me and formed me"* (NIV). Psalm 139:13 says, *"For You created my inmost being; you knit me together in my mother's womb"* (NIV). God created our children, meaning He oversaw every detail and declared their lives "good."

Saying a child with special needs has the same quality of life as a fully functioning adult may seem odd or naïve. The point here is that, while daily living may be vastly different, both individuals have the same value. Everyone has been created specifically by God and everyone has the opportunity to glorify God with his or her life, no matter what that looks like.

We also must remember that this is not mere theory or Bible doctrine. God loves us — each of us, personally — and cares about our lives. He doesn't love you or your child just because He loves everybody. He really loves you personally, and He loves your child personally. He cares about every detail of you, down to counting the hairs on your head (Matthew 10:29-31). When we search for God's perspective toward us and our children with special needs, we find many biblical truths and explanations. But we must remind ourselves above all else of His deep, personal love for us.

We can take comfort in knowing we don't have to bend to the world's ideas of success and can instead pursue our loving, caring God Who created each of us specifically. In Him, we all have the opportunity for the highest quality of life, regardless of limitations. His peace, hope, and joy make any life profoundly worth living — and are often the envy of those who have achieved worldly success but still find themselves wanting.

## GOD'S EXPECTATIONS OF US

So, what do we do with all of this? Knowing what we've learned about God and what the Bible teaches about His perspective toward us, ow do we move forward? What does God expect of us and our children?

I think one Bible verse sets the only expectation we are to place on our children with special needs, and it's not an expectation connected to unrealistic intellectual or physical milestones.

Micah 6:8 says: "He has shown you, O man, what is good; and what does the Lord require of you? But to do justly, and to love mercy, and to walk humbly with your God" (NKJV).

To be honest, I have had to settle with this myself. I am a very driven, goal-oriented person who tends to find self-worth in my accomplishments. Yet when I look in the mirror of Scripture, I am told God delights in me doing justly, loving mercy, and walking humbly with God.

When we focus on the truth of this verse — and keep in mind how God sees us — it can change our lives. First, it really simplifies things. Gone are the millions of questions and possible factors and outcomes. Second, it keeps our outlook where it needs to be: on God. While our challenges are certainly difficult and must be dealt with every day, beginning with our eyes on God has the power to change how we approach these challenges and how they affect us.

Doing justly, loving mercy, and walking humbly with our God is all about a right relationship between us and God and us and each other — the most important things in life.

## THE DIFFICULT QUESTIONS

While we've talked a lot about broad biblical concepts that help shore up our foundation, other questions remain. For those of us dealing with tough situations personally, a few more areas need to be resolved. It's OK to ask the hard questions. In fact, it's essential for our faith. Our trust in God is not about us just blindly depending on Him. He has the answers and wants us to come to Him to know Him more.

First, we need to understand two more important principles about God.

The first is that God is love. I know you've probably heard that before. It may have been what attracted you to believe in God. Yet throughout the Bible, we see every move God makes throughout history and even today is motivated by an overarching love. This love is why we can experience forgiveness of sin through Christ's sacrifice on the cross. The love God shows us is pure. There's no way any part of it could be malicious. When God allowed us to be given children with disabilities, He did not do it as a "trick." My encouragement for you is that, based on the truth that God was intimately involved in the formation of your child in the womb, and because He is motivated by love, He has an ordained purpose for your child.

The second principle, which dovetails perfectly with God being love, is that God is completely sovereign. He is all-knowing and in control. He was not surprised or caught off guard that our Jackson was born with Down syndrome. God's sovereignty means He is all-powerful, with strength and authority. He is physically stronger than any crossfit athlete. He has more authority than any world leader. He has the ability to direct and control every detail of our lives, including everything that happens with our children.

Here are a few verses that show God's incredible sovereignty.

Colossians 1:16: ***"All things have been created through Him and for Him"*** (NIV).

Isaiah 40:21-22, 28: ***"Have you not known? Have you not heard? Has it not been told you from the beginning? Have you not understood from the foundations of the earth? It is He Who sits above the circle of the earth, and its inhabitants are like grasshoppers, Who stretches out the heavens like a curtain, and spreads them out like a tent to dwell in. … Have you not known? Have you not heard? The everlasting God, the Lord, the Creator of the ends of the earth, neither faints nor is weary. His understanding is unsearchable"*** (NKJV).

This God is *intimately* involved in the makeup of your child with special needs.

God being both sovereign and loving means none of our circumstances are a surprise, and they all have great purpose. God is and always will be the God Who is in control.

Now that we've considered these principles, it is worth the time to address the question that goes through every parent's mind at some stage in the grieving process, after learning a child has a disability. I have counseled with many families, and even though the question is presented in many forms, it boils down to this: "How can a good God allow such a bad thing?"

It's a great question, and a difficult one. Just recently I sat across a table from a man as we discussed this very topic. When we search the Bible, we find two main answers.

First, we see principles such as Romans 8:28: "And we know that all things work together for good to those who love God, to those who are the called according to His purpose." Is this a cop out? How is a disability good?

One of my greatest joys is to watch Jack desire to read and write, yet one of the greatest struggles I witness every day is the amount of work and effort he has to put toward a function that others pick up much more easily. However, when comparing his struggle to the good he has brought into our lives and the lives of those around him, the good is immeasurable and easily wins out. Often, the "good" that comes from trials cannot be appraised in human terms. This is one small earthly example. We must trust that God has a greater understanding of good than we, and that He always keeps His word.

The second answer that usually surfaces as a reason for disabilities is they are a result of sin in the world. Since Adam and Eve, the gene pool has become marred and corrupted by the effects of sin. This is not to say disabilities are caused by parents' sin, but more simply: The downward spiral of the entire physical world since the first sin has led to what we see now.

Why would a good God allow such a bad thing? Many books have been written on this topic, and it is a major hurdle to overcome. If we think about the question logically, more "Why?" questions emerge. Why did God allow sin? Then, why doesn't He stop it? Why did God allow it to happen to my child?

We ultimately come to the conclusion that God hasn't told us. God says trials produce patience and endurance (James 1:2-4; Romans 5:3-5), but He hasn't told us why He allows disabilities and genetic deformities.

The difficult part is to accept this reality and still trust that God is, well, still God.

There is an account in the Bible told by the Apostle Paul in 2 Corinthians. Paul refers to some physical problem that made it difficult to function, much like a disability. He said he prayed over and over for God to take it away. God did not take it away, but He gave Paul a response that can be encouraging to us: ***"My grace is sufficient for you, for My power is made perfect in weakness"*** (2 Corinthians 12:9, NIV).

God does care for your child. He knows about his or her special needs, and God also knows that you, the parent, hurt. Sometimes the pain is almost unbearable, and you would do anything to get rid of it. God's response is a gentle encouragement to trust and rely on Him to keep us strong.

*Bobby Lanyon*

# Chapter Two

# They Found the Cure!

*Having a plan to navigate ethical
questions in the medical world*

Scientific health research took a definitive step forward in 1905, when biologist William Bateson coined the term "genetics" to describe the study of heredity and variation in living organisms.

In the time since, genetic research has been enhanced incredibly through intelligent minds and increased technology. Since 2001, we have been living in the post-genomic era, with the human genome (genetic makeup) fully mapped out so that individual genes can be isolated and studied further. The whole concept of being able to see how the body works and replicates itself on a cellular level is fascinating. It also enables medical professionals (not me — I just read a lot of study reports) to learn why different disabilities or syndromes cause certain outcomes. Currently, advanced research is focusing on the manipulation of specific genes. This is called gene therapy. The idea is that, by tweaking certain genes, when cells replicate throughout the body, they will replicate without malformations (most of which, such as those associated with disabilities, are considered negative).

All throughout history, people have been on a quest to fix things. On a spiritual level, we try to do good deeds, thinking they will help our position before God. In a practical way, we try to fix politics, national economies, or relationships. The list could go on and on. At home, we try to fix the clogged sink drain or glue the doll back together that was chewed by the dog. In our home, I am constantly rebuilding Lego sets that get destroyed. Something in the human psyche drives us to fix things. It is a noble endeavor — even God-given — to want to fix homes and cities and relationships. But when it comes to manipulating cells in our bodies, is there a boundary line we may be crossing?

A TV news station once interviewed me regarding a scientific breakthrough that would allow gene therapists to "mask" the symptoms of Down syndrome by genetically manipulating and "covering up" the extra 21st chromosome. This would be accomplished by applying the process of meiosis to the replication of the DNA. It sounded promising. It could mean stronger muscle control for internal organs and more control of gross and fine motor skills. Yet even before I finished those thoughts, I wondered how this gene manipulation would affect the people it was designed to help.

While gene manipulation is still somewhat in the future for widespread application, we parents who desire God's plan in our families must seriously analyze the moral and ethical implications of such research — and not just gene therapy, but all forms of medical research.

Please understand that I do believe medical research has an extremely important role to play in our lives. Some of our children would not even be alive today if not for the wondrous discoveries of medicine. My own son's life has been saved several times by fantastic, well-educated, passionate doctors. But just as a car is meant to stay within the confines of a road system, if we drive recklessly and with selfish human abandon with these types of ethical decisions, we can create risk and potentially harm other people.

As Christian parents, we need to be able to agree on the "means" (the methods being used) to justify the "end" (healing, cures, or relief). In order to do that, the ethical motivations and implications behind research must be clearly defined.

To keep with my example of gene therapy, it is still very unclear in the world of genetic manipulation if and where someone's personality combines with his or her physiological makeup. It's still not known if genetic manipulation could alter someone's personality. Questions like these are pertinent and need to be answered before implementation.

Psalm 139:13 tells us God Himself knit together your child in the womb. That means God was active in every detail, down to each cell, gene, or chromosome. God has all situations in His powerful, knowledgeable, capable hands.

Again, I am not discouraging any of us from taking advantage of the help we can get. To say medical research, advanced treatment, and other social or environmental therapies are all against a Christian perspective toward bioethics is absolutely ludicrous.

However, my encouragement is that, as parents, we need to become knowledgeable and discerning so we can best utilize the wonderful benefits of medical research and development. The end goal is that our children reach their potential while we are vigilant to make these decisions with an appropriate perspective of how God views and loves our children.

## HELPING OUR CHILDREN REACH THEIR POTENTIAL

Let me finish this chapter by noting that as caretakers of our children, we have a legitimate responsibility and authority to ensure they reach their potential. In Mark 2:1-11, we see men acting as family for a paralyzed man and taking him to Jesus for healing. These men purposefully acted to help the paralyzed man become what they knew he could be. Often, it can be hard to decide whether to just accept a situation or to expend energy looking for a remedy. The example here encourages us to seek healing and relief with hope.

Fellow parents, we are blessed by God to be called to proactively help our children with special needs do all they can do. So, remain at the helm. Be educated and seek guidance from people who are also educated and whom you trust. Remember to prayerfully consider therapies and medical processes as you head toward your end goal of helping your child function to his or her potential.

*Bobby Lanyon*

# Chapter Three:

# Discipline

*Why we correct our children*

For as long as I live, I will never forget when my family moved from a town called Rockhampton in Queensland, Australia, to where I was born, a small town six hours south named Dalby. At the time, I was 15 and fully devoted to playing soccer. I was a striker and was training up to four times a week. I loved soccer. I lived and breathed soccer. I played for my town at times and also toured Japan with a travel team. My aspirations were high: I wanted to play soccer for life.

My family moved just four weeks before deciding if I would travel to Germany for a monthlong training camp. I was super excited about possibly going to Germany. This camp could be the catalyst that would propel me into even more specialized training camps with scouts from teams around the world. Even before we fully settled in Dalby, I sought out the local coach and was accepted onto the team. All seemed well. I proudly returned home to inform my dad of my plans. Everything was great — that is, until it came out during the discussion that I would be playing Sunday mornings, the same time as church. This was different than my old schedule of Friday and Saturday nights.

Soccer was my dream. I enjoyed it, and I was good at it. I can't recall all the details and talks with my parents that ensued, but I remember sitting in my room looking out the window of our home on the edge of town at the small country airstrip in the fields across the street. I did not go to church, nor did I head to the soccer pitch. I knew if I chose church, my dream of grass-stained knees and switching sweaty jerseys at the end of the grand finals would never come to fruition. I was also keenly aware that if I picked soccer, I would be choosing a deliberate life endeavor apart from God's will for me.

## CHOICES AND CONSEQUENCES

I share this story to illustrate that choices always have consequences. Newton's third law of motion states that for every action, there is an equal and opposite reaction. If I had chosen soccer, I would have fed my competitive spirit and fulfilled my lifelong dream, but I wouldn't have had time for church or many other opportunities. You can't have both — a choice takes you in one direction or the other. Playing soccer was not wrong, but in this situation, it opened the way for me to make a wrong choice if I pursued it over God. My full-speed journey toward soccer stardom stopped at that point, and to this day I haven't seriously laced up a pair of cleats. I never went to that training camp in Germany. Running the sideline of a soccer pitch with the ball at my feet is simply a fond memory, and it does not bring guilt or regret because I know I made the God-honoring choice as a teenager.

Not all decisions carry moral weight. Some are innocuous: You go either this way or that, with no right or wrong motive or possible error (although the outcome of such choices can still greatly influence your life). The Bible tells us, however, that we *are* accountable for the many good and bad choices we make. Scripture clearly teaches that our choices have consequences. 2 Corinthians 5:10 says we must answer to God for those decisions:

"For we [believers will be called to account and] must all appear before the judgment seat of Christ, so that each one may be repaid for what has been done in the body, whether good or bad [that is, each will be held responsible for his actions, purposes, goals, motives — the use or misuse of his time, opportunities, and abilities]" (Amplified).

John 3:16 shows other choices and consequences. If we choose to cross the line of faith with Jesus for the forgiveness of our sins, the consequence is that we will go not to Hell, but to Heaven for eternity. The opposite is also true. If a person does not confess Jesus Christ and believe God raised Him from the dead, that person will not spend eternity in Heaven with God.

## THE PURPOSE OF DISCIPLINE

We understand these principles. But how do we convey these abstract ideas to our children, especially our children with intellectual delays? And how does this tie in with discipline?

Instead of focusing on methodology, let's look at the purpose of discipline and why our children need a solid understanding of choices and consequences. The reason I won't go into how to discipline is because the method you choose should be based on your expert knowledge of your child and how he or she responds to correction. You as the parent know best. We all need to settle within ourselves our vision and desired outcome for the discipline of our children. Having a clear purpose for discipline will help each of us determine this vision as well as our individual methodology.

Often, when we consider how and why to discipline, we only focus on a child's noncompliant behavior. Let's start by understanding that God has given us a clear purpose and desired end result for discipline, and it is not merely to correct behavior. We can get caught up in doing the actions of parenting and forget why we want to correct our children. We may do something such as discipline a child for the sake of having a quiet home, yet we miss the heart motivation or attitude behind the behavior. Discipline is not just about correcting behavior, although a child's actions certainly may change as a byproduct of steady, purpose-driven discipline.

It's worth stopping here for a moment to share a story. Sometimes, as parents of children with special needs, we have the added challenge of trying to determine whether a child is willfully misbehaving or just exhibiting involuntary actions due to a disability.

In the summer of 2015, my family was given an amazing gift and huge answer to prayer: a 9-week-old

45

Chocolate Labrador we named Jonah. We want Jonah to be a service dog for Jack, specifically to keep him safe from running and also to motivate Jack to go where we tell him to go. Jonah grew very quickly both in size and in having an incredible bond with Jack.

Sometimes, when it is time to go upstairs for bed, Jack will stop at the bottom of the stairs, flop on the floor, and refuse to go up. At first, my wife and I rationalized that because Jack has Down syndrome, he has low muscle tone, and after a long day, he is tired and just doesn't have the strength to make it up the sixteen stairs to the top. This was a normal occurrence until Jonah came along. We learned Jack *could* go up the stairs but chose not to. He had become good at playing the "can't" card. We taught Jonah to go up the stairs ahead of Jack, and very quickly, we saw Jack was sure to follow. This humorous little example taught us the difference between Jack's will and his disability. I'm sure you have examples of your own.

Back to the purpose of discipline: Godly discipline goes beyond correcting outward behavior and lays the groundwork for a changed heart — and, more important, a heart that comes to know Jesus.

This is the ultimate purpose of discipline: to point our children to God as the Savior and forgiver of sin. By teaching our children about choices and consequences, we can help them see their need for the biggest choice everyone must make. By modeling godly authority and demonstrating mercy and justice in this life, we can lead them to an understanding of God's authority and mercy, and His invitation to have a relationship with Him.

Having an end goal should encourage us. We don't have to wonder if we need a different objective because our children may not intellectually understand principles at the same age as other children. We just need to keep our purpose clearly in mind as we adapt to each child's individual needs.

## POINTING A CHILD TO GOD

Let's return to choices and consequences now that we have our purpose in mind. We ultimately want to point our children to the most important decision: choosing God and His way to an eternity with Him. To do that, we must start building an understanding of all kinds of choices and consequences. For example, we show our kids that some choices have physical consequences, such as them getting burned if they touch a hot stove or a toy breaking if they throw it during a tantrum. We also teach them how choices affect people, such as words or actions hurting others emotionally or physically. We establish authority by showing them that if they make certain decisions, we will respond a certain way, and they need to obey if they want certain results.

Teaching choices and consequences at a level our children can understand not only helps them develop behaviorally and stay safe physically but also creates a path to spiritual understanding.

When we teach our children about salvation, we will teach them that in order for us to be forgiven of our sin, we must obey God and follow His way of approaching Him, which is through Jesus Christ. Psychologically, this is an abstract concept that is difficult for young children to comprehend. However, the more we show our children examples of the need for obedience in everyday life, the easier the connection will be when we tell them they must obey God. If they understand life's "rules," we can help them grasp God's standards. Everyday choices and consequences can be building blocks toward helping them realize their need for Jesus.

The only way our children can have a relationship with God is His prescribed way of obedience. If we do not instruct, encourage, and discipline our children to obey concrete directives from parents or others in authority, they won't see the need to come to God through obedience, and they won't be able to envision God as their heavenly Father Who longs for a relationship with them. Discipline is our helper as we lead our children to an understanding of God and His loving provision for them.

## THE FRUIT OF DISCIPLINE

This view of discipline is not limited to children. In fact, the biblical principles behind these ideas apply to all believers. Hebrews 12:1-11, in teaching about discipline, says the end goal is to yield "the peaceful fruit of righteousness [right standing with God and a lifestyle and attitude that seeks conformity to God's will and purpose]" (verse 11, Amplified). God uses discipline in our lives to point us back to Him and His ways, which yield righteousness as we obey Him.

The chapter right before those verses, Hebrews 11, is full of examples of men and women who showed great faith in God. They, too, experienced discipline as

God used it to produce righteousness in their lives. These men and women had to believe in God and His promise that, even if they could not see it (Hebrews 11:39), following His way was the best choice.

We can rest in knowing that God wants what's best for us and our children as we seek to follow Him in the way we lead and correct our kids.

This book is not going to tell you how to achieve that goal. The methods you choose will be based on what you perceive your child can cognitively understand and whether you think correction will cause an adverse, negative reaction or a growing understanding of choices and consequences.

This is a slow process. At this point in our family life with Jack, we are still in the early going, and his understanding is far more rudimentary than that of his brother, who is two years younger.

Be encouraged. God does give us a great promise in Scripture. Philippians 1:6 assures us, ***"He Who has begun a good work in you will complete it until the day of Jesus"*** (NKJV).

Keep pointing your child to Jesus.

# Chapter Four:

# Friendship

*God uses relationships as
a channel of blessing*

If you've ever aimlessly scrolled through Facebook, you know the kind of quotes people like to share to describe friendship and what it means to them. I've seen many philosophical quotes, but one of my favorite comments came from author Linda Grayson: "There is nothing better than a friend, unless it's a friend with chocolate." These quotes are just one of the ways people try to explain the value of meaningful friendships. One thing is for sure — DC Talk was right when they sang, "We all wanna be loved." People long for good friendships.

My wife, Michelle, has the best friendships. She has a great disposition that attracts people to her. Even many years after elementary school, she still gets together regularly with some girlfriends she's known since childhood.

Michelle and I experienced the power of friendship in a special way when Jackson was born. When we learned Jack had Down syndrome and had been admitted to the Neonatal Intensive Care Unit, one of the first people Michelle called for support and encouragement was a friend from elementary school who works in special education. I will never forget the friend's response when Michelle told her Jack had Down syndrome. "Oh, that's all?" her friend said. "I thought something was really wrong!" Those simple words from a trusted friend gave Michelle reassurance and calm.

## SETTING THE TONE FOR SOLID FRIENDSHIPS

Children with special needs and disabilities need friends, too.

Most of us would agree we want our children to have friends. But far too often, we allow fearful thoughts into our hearts and minds that lead to decisions that can create distance between our children and their peers.

As grown and mature adults, we have a heightened understanding and fear of discrimination. We've seen it or experienced it ourselves. We live in a world tainted by sin and harmful attitudes, and the last hurt we want our children with disabilities to encounter is discrimination.

I would like us to look deeper into our own hearts, though. Sometimes, our own personal fear of being discriminated against may be what keeps us from actively seeking to cultivate friendships for our children. Some of us would do almost anything to avoid someone treating *us* that way, and we carry that into how we parent. When we impose such fears onto our children's relationships, we only feed this world's ongoing cycles of prejudice, stereotyping, and discrimination.

In many ways, we set the tone for discrimination by how we treat our children. Consciously or not, we are examples for others. We fear our children may be "labeled" or won't be able to keep up. Then we assume that because they can't keep up in a game of tag, they are not having fun. I have even seen situations where children with disabilities don't get appropriate education because their parents "feel" the people responsible at schools or daycare environments are not caring or educated enough to modify activities for an inclusive environment.

However, this has a good side, too. You will often find that people treat your child the way you treat him or her. Think about it for a moment. Your child's peers and their parents most likely do not have the constant exposure to disabilities that you have. Because they don't have this experience, they legitimately do not have the knowledge to respond appropriately. We have the opportunity to set the tone for constructive behavior by how we treat our children and model ways to help them. Rather than being driven by fear of discrimination, we can choose to be motivated by hope toward positive attitudes. Many people we connect with are blank slates when it comes to interacting with children with special needs. We can literally change our world's patterns of discrimination, prejudice, and stereotyping by offering a new perspective for these people's first encounter with disabilities.

I remember taking Jack to a birthday party for one of his first grade friends. It was a football party. When we arrived, there was loud music and kids playing football. Very quickly, Jack shut down. I tried all the motivational tricks I knew with no success. The mother of the birthday boy asked if she could do anything to help. I asked if she could simply turn down the music because I could tell the noise was over-stimulating to

Jack. She had no idea how to help, but with my suggestion, she graciously turned off the music. After a few minutes, Jack was able to focus and began running around the makeshift football field with the other 6-year-old boys.

When it comes to creating and facilitating relationships for our kids with special needs, we need to be the ones who will foster the understanding that friends and parents will act on. When I took Jack to that party, I was the only one there who knew Jack does not respond well to loud environments. Does that mean Jack's friends were wrong to play loud music outside? Not at all. They were innocently ignorant, and once we talked about the situation, they were more than willing to do whatever was necessary to remove the stimuli so Jack could function and enjoy the party. You, as the parent of your child with special needs, will always be the cheerleader for education and opportunities, and you will also be the educator to help facilitate your child's social environment.

Additionally, our children's peers often want them to be involved. They get a sense of fulfillment from helping our kids discover and experience what everyone else is experiencing. It's our privilege to enable them to do that.

## THE VALUE OF FRIENDSHIP

We know from our own life experience how special and important friendships can be. Something interesting to be aware of, though, is that research has also found an empirical value to relationships. Peer-to-peer friendships are actually an incredible motivator and tool for our kids to develop tangible skills for life.

Here is some great insight from one of the best occupational therapists I have had the privilege of knowing and serving with, Kelly Nelson:

*As a pediatric occupational therapist, parents often ask me what toys they should purchase to increase their child's developmental skills. There are so many wonderful toys, including building sets, puzzles, and Playdough, which promote fine motor, gross motor, and language skills. However, the best investment is not in toys, but in activities that promote friendship. Friendships are essential to a child's health and development. During play with peers, children practice skills like problem solving, communication, and cooperation, all of which are necessary for success later in life. Friendships can lead to greater involvement in school and higher self-esteem (Ladd, Kochenderfer, & Coleman 1996).*

*Research suggests that friendships not only increase social emotional skills but can also have a positive impact on physical health. Studies have demonstrated that children are highly motivated and will engage in physical activity for longer periods of time if engaging in that activity with a friend (Barkley et al 2014, Salvy et al 2009). Friendships also play a role in language development. When involved in play with highly expressive peers, children gain insight into language skills and increase expressive communication (Mashburn et al 2009). Friendships not only enhance a child's abilities, but they can also prevent stress and anxiety. Dr. William M. Bukowski and his colleagues found that having just one friend can prevent depression and isolation in school-age children (Bukowski, Laursen, & Hoza 2010).*

*With such overwhelming evidence of the benefits of friends, parents should consider investing in play dates and social activities to be a vital component to their child's success.*

## THE BIBLE'S BACKING FOR FRIENDSHIP

That friendships produce such positive outcomes makes perfect sense. It also makes sense, then, if we look to the Bible, that God has a purpose for friendship.

Foundationally, Genesis 2:18 tells us, "It is not good for [a] man to be alone" (NIV). We are meant to have friends. While this verse is typically used when talking about marriage, the same biblical principle applies to all relationships. God created us as relational beings, and all the different types of relationships in life show our same basic need for connection.

Ecclesiastes 4:9-12, another well-known passage about relationships, is also applicable as we think about our children's friendships:

*"Two are better than one,*

*Because they have a good reward for their labor.*

*For if they fall, one will lift up his companion.*

*But woe to him who is alone when he falls,*

*For he has no one to help him up.*

*Again, if two lie down together, they will keep warm;*

*But how can one be warm alone?*

*Though one may be overpowered by another, two can withstand him.*

*And a threefold cord is not quickly broken."* (NKJV)

### Here is the series of principles:

Verse 9 — There is productivity in friendship. When two friends work together, they can accomplish more toward their common goal. They have a greater benefit than if they worked alone.

One of the coolest moments parents who take advantage of inclusive education models get to experience is watching their children learn to read, count, and solve problems together. The kids learn so much more — and benefit in other ways — than when trying to learn on their own. This happens in classrooms or church environments whenever a group of children is together.

Verse 10 — There is accountability in friendship. A friend looks out for his or her friend. Children who grow up in environments where they experience social etiquette are shown what behavior is appropriate and what is not by their friends. When we allow our children with special needs to have friendships with other children, they are held accountable to learn how to interact.

I remember an encouraging moment when watching Jack sit on his Curious George chair mat during circle time in his classroom. He had been sitting with his classmates for almost four minutes, so the fidgeting began. Without any prompting, a young girl shuffled over, sat next to Jack, and told him to look at the teacher. She knew what to do to keep him accountable.

Verse 11 — There is intimacy in friendship. When cold seasons of life blow in and bring discouragement, it is comforting and reassuring to have friends who give us the warmth to make it through. At this point, we probably need to remember that friendships are not always mutually giving. Certain times in everyone's life require friends to give without receiving.

I will never forget the hot September day when I was in the middle of a very difficult time at my job. I had made few sales, and my employer would have been completely justified to let me go. Just when I thought things could not get worse, I was told another client had canceled its very large order. Needless to say, I had nothing to give to anyone. In desperate hopelessness, I left the office and drove to the only place in the world I feel safe: home. I got there just as Jack was finishing his nap. As we walked down the stairs together, he pulled at me to sit on the steps. Halfway down the stairs we sat, and he folded his hands over my shoulder and proceeded to pray. Words were not important. I was in tears. How could a 4-year-old be so perceptive and encouraging to show such love and warmth at a time when I was truly out in the cold by myself? God uses friendship as a channel for blessing.

Verse 12 — There is protection in friendship. This principle can truly dispel our parental fears. If social media has shown us anything about special needs, it's that in the majority of situations, friends protect their friends with disabilities. There will always be people who think individuals with special needs should not be included. We can pray for those people, because they most likely have not experienced biblical friendships with anyone, let alone someone with special needs. And we can expect our children's peers to stick up for our kids. We have seen this in Jack's life, and you may have experienced it as well.

## THE GREATER PURPOSE

You may have noticed that all these principles include characteristics of God. Realizing this gives this passage its greatest impact. When we encourage our children to form friendships with their peers, we are essentially making a way for them to show God to others. God will use our children with special needs to bless their friends. Even more, we are also enabling our children's friends to be a witness and blessing of God, and we're allowing God to bless our children through these friends.

The purpose of friendship is for God to bless one individual via another person and vice versa.

Why would we let our parental fears inhibit such blessing to others and even our own children? God very rarely sends physical manna from Heaven to sustain us. More often, He works through the people and situations in our lives to fulfill His promise of providing for our every need. In this case, God has given our children friends so He can use our kids as conduits for blessing others, and so others can be used by God to bless our children. With this purpose in mind, we can look around our educational, sporting, and church social circles to see where we can practically get our children plugged in to create friendships filled with blessings from God.

*Bobby Lanyon*

# Chapter Five:

# Marriage

*Communication. Communication.*
*Communication.*

All day, every day, our eyes and ears are bombarded by things that need our attention — from our responsibilities at home and work to checking the calendar to making sure laundry gets done, people and animals are fed, and bills get paid. Nowhere on that list is any reference to your spouse. That's just what you have to do for yourself and others who rely on you.

I often wonder how Dad and Mum managed to raise me and my three siblings between school, sports, and social activities. They somehow kept the house clean and put meals on the table. I never heard them complain, and they always encouraged us as they remained industrious in their own responsibilities. In fact, looking back on my life, I actually wonder if they ever slept.

But yet, growing up, we could all make our beds and do our chores (willingly or unwillingly) without super-close supervision. This is not the case in homes where a child has a disability. Our Jack is a "runner," and he's quite good at it. We've had to install latches and alarms on all our doors as well as childproof latches on the gates in the backyard. We always need to know where Jack is because we don't ever want to lose him (again). We're not concerned when we hear him playing the piano or banging blocks together. I'm sure you can relate. It's when there's no sound that our sixth sense kicks into gear, and we immediately ask, "Where's Jack?" One time I asked that question and, after a prompt reconnaissance effort, quickly pulled him back from the second floor window he had opened and was proceeding to go through. He made it halfway.

A lot of times we find ourselves fulfilling our regular parenting responsibilities and chores, and then, in addition, also working on feeding tubes, ferrying a child to therapy sessions and/or specialist visits, and on and on. Then, to make sure our typically developing children get the attention they need and deserve, we find a minute to sneak out for ice cream or some other "quality time" activity.

What happens to husband and wife time? I don't mean after the kids go to sleep (maybe) and you are in the same room, one folding laundry and the other paying bills so you can get it done and zombie your way to bed.

How marriages fare when a child has a disability is a major topic of discussion among those dealing with special needs. One often-circulated statistic is that 80% of marriages with a child with special needs end in divorce. That statistic has been proven not to have any research backing, but the sentiment rings true. Parents of children with disabilities don't have to be convinced that the divorce rate for their group is high, and many wonder how any couple can emerge from the challenges they face without eventually fracturing.

Does this have to be? I believe no, and I believe God says no, too. God has given us the tools we need to fight for our marriages, no matter what trials we encounter.

Before we move on, if you are reading this and have experienced the ruins of a fractured marriage or are a single parent of a child with special needs, I want to encourage you to hold tight to Jesus. The Bible often describes Jesus as a refuge — a strong tower and One

Who takes our burdens. Flying solo against the headwinds of special needs parenting is an amazing task. Be encouraged that there are people around you cheering you on, and God is ready to hold you up and be that listening ear when you need it — no matter what time of day or night.

## THE IMPORTANCE OF COMMUNICATION

Where does the disconnect that leads to divorce start? Most often, the breakdown begins on the communication level. In all relationships, not just marriages, distance and distrust form when the lines of communication are not utilized.

In his book *Love and Respect*, Emerson Eggerichs says miscommunication between a husband and a wife can happen simply because a man speaks through a blue megaphone and a woman hears with pink ears, and vice versa. You might be reading this with pink ears. If so, know it was written with a blue megaphone.

It's true — communication fails whenever we misinterpret words or body language. Such misinterpretation happens all the time, especially when we're busy. With all the responsibilities we have fighting for our attention, it's understandable that we struggle to communicate effectively with our spouse. The best way to combat this is to make a point to communicate often.

Something my wife and I constantly have to work at is purposefully communicating. One benefit we have is we learned early to do whatever it takes to communicate. Because we dated in the early 2000s, we didn't have reliable Internet, and phone calls were expensive, especially for poor Bible college students. Michelle and I were still in the letter-writing era. We had to make time to sit down and write to each other. Each week I would pen a five-page letter and mail it across the Pacific Ocean from Australia to Pennsylvania. It would take a week to get to Michelle. Fourteen years later, we have learned to squeeze in communication whenever we can, and even now, we find time to sit on the porch in the cool of the evening or in bed at night and just share.

I've noticed that when I do not exercise this habit, we both kick into "do" mode. We just "do" parenting. We just "do" marriage. Have you been through these motions? Are you there right now? The survival walls creep up, and it takes all we have to stop them.

This survival attitude we default to can be tricky to identify in the beginning, but some of the thoughts we have are:

"Why isn't she making sure…"

"He didn't even pick up… He is only concerned for…"

"I feel like I'm the only one who is…"

No excuses here, husband or wife. We all do it. With this in mind, let's consider 1 Peter 5:6-7:

**"Therefore humble yourselves under the mighty hand of God, that He may exalt you in due time. Casting all your care upon Him, for He cares for you"** (NKJV).

Parenting a child with a disability can be — no, *is* — exhausting! If you are reading this uninterrupted, that's a luxury.

1 Peter 5:6-7 is an amazing promise that invites us to cast our burdens on the Lord. God says we can rely on Him. We can be honest that this responsibility of raising and teaching a child with special needs is really difficult. Admit it. According to these verses, God cares for you and wants to hear about the absolute pain and

burden in your heart. He wants to hear that you really struggle sometimes.

## THE IMPORTANCE OF HUMILITY

What's interesting to see in 1 Peter 5:6-7 is the unique prerequisite: We *must humble* ourselves before God.

Humility is not our default. In fact, it's the opposite of how we usually handle things. As very capable human beings, we have a tendency to believe (and act on this belief) that we can do everything by ourselves with the talent God has given us. This leads to a frenetic lifestyle of work and activity that has us running like hamsters in a hamster wheel. Also, our culture tells us that the success *we* create determines our self-worth and identity. These mindsets do not welcome humility.

Focusing so much on success and getting things done has a price. Living this way brings compassion fatigue, crusty emotional scales across our hearts, and overactive minds that take the joy out of being a parent and make us devoid of meaningful attachment. By trying to do everything ourselves and striving to be successful, we often fail at the most important relational aspects of being human. "Survival mode" shuts out the people we want to help most, and it keeps *them* from helping *us* with their love and support.

The reality is we should not think so highly of ourselves. The Bible tells us in 2 Corinthians 4:7 that we are like a pottery jar. A pottery jar is good for one thing: holding water. We were not created with the capacity to be the ultimate sustainer of our lives and duties, nor are we intended to be the fulfillment when it comes to family, work, or responsibilities. Those roles are satisfied by the water. In completing the analogy, 2 Corinthians 4:7 says, "But we have this treasure in earthen vessels, that the excellence of the power may be of God and not of us." Christ is the water — the fulfillment and sustainer of our family, work, and responsibilities. He will take care of the people around us and all they need. We are merely the vessel He works through. It's not our job to get it all done.

The beauty of humility is we don't diminish what we can do when we put God first. Rather, we gain in what can get done in our lives, because now it's Christ's much greater power doing the work. As for being successful, 1 Peter 5:6 promises we'll be exalted if we exalt God first. When we humble ourselves and stop chasing the perpetual cycle of empty success, we open the way for God to work and for us to have a much more people-focused, compassionate lifestyle that will ultimately make us better parents and spouses. We can't be everything for everyone — especially in our own power. But when we humble ourselves before God, we make ourselves, like a pottery jar, available for Him to be what others need through us.

## THE IMPORTANCE OF BEING A TEAM

Humility is not just between us and God. We also must practice it with each other. My encouragement to all of us is to remember that as husband and wife, you are a team. You *can* be a team. You are *designed* to be a team. The Bible is telling us in 1 Peter 5:6-7 that we need to get off our soapbox, which we naturally and self-righteously go to in times of pressure and anxiety, and remember we are in the trenches together, parenting a child who has special needs.

Part of humbling ourselves and being a team is being willing to open up about insufficiencies and shortcomings. This brings us back to communication. There is safety and security in a marriage when its members are transparent about their struggles. Communicating candidly fosters an awesome bond and trust between a husband and a wife as they work together to honor the Lord as parents.

I would also like to suggest that in some cases, the person in a relationship who begins to shut down in the area of communication is the one struggling the most. It could be sin we don't want our spouse to know, or a struggle we don't know how to verbalize.

In the book I mentioned earlier, *Love and Respect*, the author puts forth the challenge that the person in the relationship who sees themselves as the most mature should be the one to make the first move toward reconciliation. It takes great strength to be humble and reach out when action is needed.

We also need to realize that our spouse may not be able to share or even understand the emotions that come with being a parent of a child with a disability. Often, half of the battle is not knowing what's going on inside ourselves. We won't always feel the same way as our spouse, and every person deals with struggles differently. We have to guard against ill will. That includes the little, everyday things we might wish were different. I love my wife, yet as I put this together, she is sleeping with Jack so he will calm down enough to sleep — not even in our bed with me. Do I like it? Not really. But I would much rather everyone get sleep so tomorrow will have at least some chance of success.

The bottom line is that as parents, you are in this together. Humility in practice is not to justify yourself or judge another but rather to serve each other, even at times when it may not be required or even when all we want to do is check out for a few minutes and leave it to the other one. Humility is a commitment to serve others like Jesus served us by selflessly giving of Himself and dying for our choice to sin.

## SHARING WHEN SOLUTIONS ARE FEW

Humility also requires us to come to grips with grieving our preconceived plans for life. It's no secret that before our children with disabilities were born, we didn't foresee the challenges and details destined for us. We probably daydreamed of an easy life — sunny days when our kids could run all over the playground and look back with big smiles filled with joy and growing independence. Be aware that if you harbor resentment about your child's disability, it will negatively affect your marriage (not to mention yourself or your relationship with your child). As children, we all learned that "honesty is the best policy." It's true. By being honest and open with your spouse, you begin to work through the confusions and pain. In the previous chapter, we saw that friends provide strength when we are weak. Sharing openly allows that principle to be applied in your marriage. It is worth noting that these conversations are not "one and done." I still have times that, if I'm completely honest, I've had to open up to Michelle about my resentment toward Jack's diagnosis, especially after a long period of Jack exhibiting noncompliant behavior at school or home.

Honest sharing is vital when it comes to the heaviest, deepest questions and insecurities we face as parents of children with special needs. Let's look at a couple more areas that can be difficult.

Having a child with a disability can be especially hard for parents who are "fix-it" people. We can generalize and say this is usually dads, but some moms are this way, too. These parents tend to focus on action and taking care of problems. Usually, they are very good at fixing whatever is going on around them. But a child with special needs presents challenges and uncertainties unlike anything they've ever encountered.

A child with a disability cannot be "fixed." If there was an easy therapy or instant cure, we would have found it. Instead, we are each facing the reality that our child is dealing with extensive, complicated problems that don't have simple solutions. My son Jack has an extra copy of the 21st chromosome in every single cell in his entire body. I cannot fix it, cure it, or make it go away. I cannot take away the intellectual disability nor the physical delay.

This is such a struggle for those of us who are fix-it parents, especially dads. Dads are macho and love to fix things on their own. We are more than content to change the oil in the car, fix the dishwasher, or plunge the toilet. The flip side is we are baffled when we're told a solution isn't needed, such as in conversations with our wives. They tell us we're just supposed to "listen" and not suggest answers or fixes — which makes *no* logical sense to us. Fixing a problem provides closure and completeness. It allows us, literally, to forget about the situation and move on.

This can never happen when you have a child with a disability. The challenges are never finished, the answers never complete. Every parent has had that great day when progress really seems to be happening. Then it's followed by a setback or a series of days that make you wonder if "progress" is a real thing. You can never forget about your child's special needs or everything that has to be done every day just to function.

When dads, or any parent, cannot fix something, it is more than understandable that insecurity sets in and questions of self-worth arise. Is it easier to just not see the situation that can't be fixed? Some people seem to think so. It's sad, but please understand their logic with compassion. It's not that these parents don't love their children. Rather, the immense mountain of overcoming their reality may be too difficult to conquer.

Parents who are good at compartmentalizing also deal with this. These people — also often dads — have this great mental ability to separate situations and experiences into different sections of their brain. If they have a sensitive conversation before work, once they get to work, they file it away and don't even think about it until work is done and they get home. Everything has its place. They file relationships, sports, work, finances, church, and God into different areas and can easily close one file drawer completely before opening another. This filing system is created from experience, and they go to each drawer based on the situation and decision they need to make.

This gift has one major problem: Disabilities don't fit any classification. What is a clear-thinking, objective, logical dad supposed to do with his precious child, whom deep down he loves like crazy, who lives with a disability the dad has no experience with and therefore no idea how to classify in his system of dealing with life?

My hypothesis is this: Dads struggle with their beloved child having a disability because they are helpless to fix the situation and have no idea how to cope with it. This affects dads emotionally and psychologically — some so greatly that daily function is dramatically inhibited.

So, in some cases, the number of which is growing, fathers are leaving their families because they seemingly have no solution. The best option in their minds is to remove the contention — by leaving their home and tearing apart a marriage and a family.

## A GREATER PURPOSE AND VALUE

Part of the trouble we have when dealing with all of this is the matter of perspective. As we struggle to classify it all in our brains or "fix it," we miss seeing the worth God says is already there.

In some cases, the only way to fix or classify something is to identify its worth. Our children have worth that is primarily assigned to them by God, not by our knowledge or experiences.

We've already seen in previous chapters that our children have great value and were created specifically by God. Let's think about one more idea. John 9:1-3 talks about a boy who was born blind.

"Now as Jesus passed by, He saw a man who was blind from birth. And His disciples asked Him, saying, 'Rabbi, who sinned, this man or his parents, that he was born blind?' Jesus answered, 'Neither this man nor his parents sinned, but that the works of God should be revealed in him'" (NKJV).

Jesus was telling His disciples that this man — far from living an inferior life, and far from being defined by sin or the effects of sin — had great worth. Even more, his life, and disability, were laying the way for God to be glorified specifically in his experience.

The same is true of our children. They have great purpose and value, and they are defined not by any diagnosis, but by God. Not all that is broken in this world is meant to be fixed by our standards, and the Bible is one shining example after another that God uses the broken, weak, and stumbling of this life to bring people to Himself on our way to the next.

We must remind ourselves how God sees us and our children whenever we feel discouraged by the parts of life we can't categorize or fix. Knowing God's perspective is the only thing that will keep us from being overwhelmed by our human view.

As for being parents, we need to come to the point where we are OK with not knowing how to solve every problem or situation. We must be open about our struggles with our spouse, which, again, brings us back to willfully choosing an attitude of humility before God. This will bring peace as we allow God to be the sovereign and loving God we know He is.

Casting Crowns' 2014 song "Broken Together" is lyrically fantastic in describing our need for humility toward each other. The chorus says:

*"Maybe you and I were never meant to be complete*
*Could we just be broken together*

*If you can bring your shattered dreams and I'll bring mine*

*Could healing still be spoken and save us*

*The only way we'll last forever is broken together."*

If you're anything like me, you might find a tear in your eye and resolve in your heart to be humble with your spouse to make your marriage strong.

# Epilogue

# Tomorrow

*Tomorrow is God's responsibility*

I would like to encourage you with one last principle as I finish this book. So far, we have taken a look at how God views our children with special needs. We spent some time thinking about having a framework of biblical bioethics. We also looked at God's design and purpose for discipline and friendship, and we saw they point us and our children back to Jesus. On the heels of being challenged to fight for our marriages, I would like you to remember that God is not absent from our lives. He is very interested in the daily events of your life. Perhaps it would be best to just let Jesus do the talking on this one.

"Therefore I tell you, do not be anxious about your life, what you will eat or what you will drink, nor about your body, what you will put on. Is not life more than food, and the body more than clothing? Look at the birds of the air: They neither sow nor reap nor gather into barns, and yet your heavenly Father feeds them. Are you not of more value than they? And which of you by being anxious can add a single hour to his span of life? And why are you anxious about clothing? Consider the lilies of the field, how they grow: They neither toil nor spin, yet I tell you, even Solomon in all his glory was not arrayed like one of these. But if God so clothes the grass of the field, which today is alive and tomorrow is thrown into the oven, will He not much more clothe you, O you of little faith? Therefore do not be anxious, saying, 'What shall we eat?' or 'What shall we drink?' or 'What shall we wear?' For the Gentiles seek after all these things, and your heavenly Father knows that you need them all. But seek first the kingdom of God and His righteousness, and all these things will be added to you.

Therefore do not be anxious about tomorrow, for tomorrow will be anxious for itself. Sufficient for the day is its own trouble" (Matthew 6:25-34, ESV).

My encouragement to you is to place that truth from God at the forefront of your mind. Making a constant effort to remember God is concerned about every part of our emotional, psychological, and physical life will, in turn, help us to rely on Him in the areas of life we have discussed in this book.

*Epilogue*

My hope is that as you have read this, you have been encouraged. It is my prayer that you will keep it as a resource to come back to when you need to refocus in the ever-hectic world of parenting a child with a disability. If this book has been an encouragement to you, consider sharing it with someone on a similar journey.

Be encouraged,


Jack's dad

*Bobby Lanyon*

# Bibliography

CHAPTER 4

Barkley JE, Salvy SJ, Sanders GJ, Dey S, Von Carlowitz KP, Williamson ML. Peer influence and physical activity behavior in young children: an experimental study. J Phys Act Health. 2014 Feb; 11(2): 404-9.

Ladd GW, Kochenderfer BJ, Coleman CC. Friendship quality as a predictor of young children's early school adjustment. Child Dev. 1996 Jun; 67(3): 1103-18.

Mashburn, A. J., Justice, L. M., Downer, J. T. and Pianta, R. C. (2009), Peer Effects on Children's Language Achievement During Pre-Kindergarten. Child Development, 80: 686-702.

Salvy SJ, Roemmich JN, Bowker JC, Romero ND, Stadler PJ, Epstein LH. Effect of peers and friends on youth physical activity and motivation to be physically active. J Pediatr Psychol. 2009 Mar; 34(2): 217-25.

William M. Bukowski, Brett Laursen and Betsy Hoza (2010). The snowball effect: Friendship moderates escalations in depressed affect among avoidant and excluded children. Development and Psychopathology, 22, pp 749-757.

J Pediatr Nurs. 2006 Aug; 21(4): 299-307.

CHAPTER 5

Eggerichs, Emerson. Love and Respect. Nashville: Thomas Nelson, 2004.

All Scripture is from the New International Version (NIV), New King James Version (NKJV), English Standard Version (ESV), or Amplified Bible.

For more information contact:

Bobby Lanyon
C/O Advantage Books
P.O. Box 160847
Altamonte Springs, FL 32716

info@advbooks.com

To purchase additional copies of this book visit our bookstore website at: www.advbookstore.com

Longwood, Florida, USA
"we bring dreams to life"™
www.advbookstore.com

CPSIA information can be obtained at www.ICGtesting.com
Printed in the USA
BVOW06s0855050916

460687BV00004B/6/P